VEDANTA

VEDANTA

Karan Singh

Rupa & Co

© Karan Singh 1996
First published 1996 by Rupa & Co.
Second impression 2001
7/16 Ansari Road, Daryaganj, New Delhi 110 002.
Printed in India by Gopsons Papers Ltd., A-14, Sector 60, Noida 201 301

ISBN 81-7167-347-3

Cover and inside design: Supriya S. Lamba

Preface

We live in an age of turmoil, tension and transition. The old is collapsing and the new is struggling to be born, and we find ourselves adrift on a turbulent ocean with no established landmarks between the vanished past and an indeterminate future. There are of course new hopes and fresh aspirations throughout the world, and there is also a tremendous quest for light and for inner guidance, particularly among young people. At such a juncture, we look into our spiritual and cultural heritage, not in order to go back, but for the light, inspiration and courage to go forwards into the future with clarity and confidence.

Hinduism has a unique corpus of wisdom going back unbroken for thousands of years to the very dawn of history. There were older civilizations, but they are not living any longer. You can go to Egypt and see the pyramids and sphinx, but you cannot contact that civilization because it is dead. With the Indian civilization you can go back all the way to the Vedas because it is still a living, a continuing, and a dynamic flow.

Hinduism is unique in several respects. It is the only religion in the world which is not based either on any specific text, or on the teachings of any particular person or in any specific point in time. All the other religions of the world, without exception, trace their teachings back to a single individual, therefore to a single text and therefore to a single point in time. It is not so for Hinduism. There is a pluralism which is built into the very structure of Hindu thought, because it is based on the collective wisdom of seers and sages, or the *Rishis,* and these great utterances have come down to us over many thousands of years and remain a source of great inspiration.

The Vedas can be likened to the Himalayas, that mighty mountain range described by the great Poet Kalidasa in the opening verse of *Kumarsambhava* as a great spiritual presence that stretches from the West to the Eastern sea like a measuring rod to gauge the greatness of the world's civilisations. As the Himalayas have been the source of our great rivers, of our civilisation, in the same way the whole Vedic Corpus stands as the great Himalayas of the mind. They consist of hundreds of thousands of verses which have come down through the centuries entirely by ear, a mnemonic feat unrivalled in human history. They contain the most beautiful verses addressed to different aspects of the divinity, with or without form. "Aum. O worshipful ones, with our ears may we hear what is auspicious, may we, efficient in worship, see with our eyes what is auspicious. May we singing your praise, live our allotted span of life with strong limbs and healthy bodies."

If we look upon the Vedas as the Himalayas, then the Upanishads can be likened to those great Himalayan peaks clothed in eternal snow and bathed in the glory of sunshine, standing in grandeur and tremendous beauty. The Upanishads are known as the Vedanta, the 'end' of the Vedas, both because chronologically they come at the end of the Vedic collections, and also because they represent the high watermark of Vedic thought.

Traditionally there are believed to be 108 Upanishads, but Adi Shankaracharya, the great philosopher to whom we owe a great deal of our understanding of the Upanishads, commented upon eleven—the Isha, the Kena, the Katha, the Prashna, the Mundaka, the Mandukya, the Taittiriya, the Aitaraiya, the Chhandogya, the Brihadaranyaka and the Shwetashwatára. The Upanishads are dialogues between the teacher and one or more pupils, very much like Socratic dialogue. For a parallel to the western tradition, the Upanishads would be like the Socratic Dialogues plus the Old Testament. It has been said that the whole of Western philosophy is a series of footnotes to Plato. It could perhaps be said that the whole of Eastern philosophy is a series of footnotes to the Upanishads, because all the great streams of thought that subsequently developed find their origin in them. These dialogues range from very short cryptic texts—the Mandukya has 12 verses, the Ishavasya which is considered perhaps the most important, has only 18—all the way to the great Chhandogya and Brihadaranyaka Upanishads which have many hundreds of verses.

The word 'Upanishad' has two meanings, one is 'sitting down near' and describes the disciples sitting around a Guru as he expounds the science of Brahman. Another meaning is 'the secret doctrine' or 'the saving wisdom', as the Upanishads deal with esoteric teachings which require a deep inner desire to absorb the high teachings. In the Upanishads we come across an extraordinary galaxy of remarkable human beings, Gurus as well as disciples. There is Yama himself, the God of Death, Yajnyavalkya, who was the greatest philosopher of his times, King Janaka, who is known as the Rajarshi, Angirasa, Ashtavakr and other great teachers. There are also many great pupils, the boy Nachiketa who confronts Yama in the Kathopanishad and asks him certain searching questions, Shwetaketu, Shaunaka the great householder, Gargi, a woman who takes a very active role in the Brihadaranyaka Upanishad with her husband Yajnavalkya. So the Upanishads are a series of extraordinary dialogues, of brilliant and inspiring texts.

It is particularly interesting that as the globalisation of consciousness speeds up, as it has done in the last few decades over which we have become technologically very much one world, the teachings of the Vedanta become increasingly relevant. This is the true test of a scripture. If it is not relevant to us today, then it is purely archival, useful for scholars of theology or philosophy but with no immediacy for us in our daily lives no impact upon our consciousness, upon the way we react to our environment and with fellow human beings.

The spiritual teachings are not simply meant for the mind, they are not intellectual gymnastics, they appeal to the deeper reaches of the human personality, to the sub-conscious and the super-conscious mind, to the emotions, to the heart. It is a great mistake to approach the Vedantic philosophy purely as an academic exercise. In Hinduism the word for philosophy is *Darshana,* which comes from *drishya,* meaning to see, "Where the mind falls back along with words, unable to attain." The ultimate realisation is something which cannot be verbalised, and yet we have to use words as the creative link between higher consciousness and us, between our normal consciousness and the higher reaches of consciousness which are dealt within all the esoteric teachings of the world including the Upanishads.

It is very difficult to summarise the Upanishads,

because they are so profound and vast. But there are some seminal concepts from the Upanishads which are particularly relevant to us in the present day and age. The first and the most fundamental teaching of the Vedanta is the all pervasiveness of the divine. Everything that exists, wherever it exists is permeated by the divine, not only this tiny speck of dust that we call planet Earth, but the billions upon billions of galaxies in the unending universe around us—"that which, shining, causes everything else to shine", in other words the light of consciousness itself, that is the Brahman and that is all pervasive. The concept of the all pervasive Brahman represents, perhaps, the philosophical correlate to the Unified Field Theory which scientists are trying to find, because they are also looking for a single force that can explain the entire manifestation, the entire cosmos. In the concept of the Brahman of the

Upanishads we already have the philosophical basis of this concept, that whatever exists, wherever it exists, whether it has manifested or not manifested, or whether it will manifest in the future, is all permeated by the divine. That is why this magnificent universe around us is not something to be in any way denigrated. The seers sing in ecstasy about this glory of consciousness, the glory of the universe. Life-negating philosophies seem to think that the universe itself is a terrible mistake that should never have occurred. This is not accepted by the Vedanta. The Vedanta has a very positive attitude towards the universe. And if the Brahman is the reality, then the universe which is the manifestation of that reality also needs to be nurtured. So the first and perhaps most fundamental concept of the Vedanta is the unity of all existence, the all pervasiveness of the divine.

The second is the potential divinity inherent in each human being. The human being in Vedanta is looked upon not as some kind of a creature crawling on the earth in fear and trembling, but as being endowed by the very fact of consciousness with essential divinity. The Upanishads have a marvellous term for the human race—Children of Immortality—because we encapsulate in our being the possibility of divine realisation. This is a concept that cuts across all barriers and endows every human being ever born on this planet, now or in the future, with a dignity which is unique because each human being has the capacity for spiritual growth and spiritual development.

The dignity of the individual human being rests upon this concept of the Vedanta that there is a divine spark in each person, called the *Atman*. So you have the *Brahman* which is pervading the entire universe, and the *Atman* which is the divinity manifested in each individual, and joining the *Brahman* and the *Atman* is the supreme goal of human life and endeavour. Fanning the spark of spiritual consciousness into the blazing fire of spiritual realisation is the great challenge and opportunity offered to us by the Vedanta. This joining of the *Atman* and the *Brahman* is what is known as Yoga. The word 'yoga' comes from the same root as the English word 'yoke', which means to join, and yoga is the process which joins the divinity within us with the all pervasive divinity around us, God immanent and God transcendent.

Briefly, there are four main paths of yoga in the Hindu tradition. There is a *Jnana Yoga*, the way of wisdom, which in the West would be the way of Plato, the contemplation of the eternal truths, the archetypes that stand behind our consciousness.

There is the *Bhakti Yoga*, the way of devotion, of an outpouring of love to a personalised aspect of the divine, which in the West would be like Saint Francis of Assisi, St Teresa of Avila or St John on the Cross, a tremendous devotional outpouring. There is the *Karma Yoga*, the way of works dedicated to the divine, in the West again it would be the way of Martha, the way good works as against the way of Mary which is devotion. And then there is the *Raja Yoga*, the royal path, which is the way of spiritual practices and disciplines which enable us to elevate our consciousness. That is the way of great western mystics, of Meister Ekhart and Ruysbroeck, of the great Sufis like Maulana Jalaluddin Rumi who have drunk the wine of divinity. This path includes breathing meditational practices which enable us to elevate our consciousness.

There is the all pervasive Brahman, the Atman

within and the methodology of joining them which is Yoga. The third Vedantic concept is the remarkable vision of the entire human race as a single extended family—*vasudhaiva kutumbakam*. This cuts across all barriers of race or religion, of caste or creed, of language or nationality, of sex or social status, all barriers that divide human beings are transcended in this concept of the world as a family. As we hurtle towards the end of this millennium, we find that science and technology in fact have brought this about. A television set immediately makes us a participant in global consciousness. We are no longer confined to our own time or to our own place, we become global citizens. If we are to develop a harmonious and sane world order, then at some level we have to accept this over-riding unity. Religion, race or nationality are certainly important, but ultimately you cannot divide the human race on the basis of these different concepts. You have to unify them, and the unifying factor can only be the spiritual spark in all human beings. That is the golden thread that binds together people of diverse creeds and backgrounds, and this is a very important element in the emerging global society.

Global consciousness which is now emerging has got to accept on the one hand the multiplicity of our cultural heritage, and on the other hand the underlying unity of the entire human race. This Vedantic concept is in fact post-modern, because we are still stuck in many of the pre-global concepts. We look upon ourselves as being essentially distinct due to the situation of our birth, religion, nationality, race or sex and are tied down by these accidents of birth. But the deeper element of the unity underlying the human race is something which is only now beginning to be understood, though yet imperfectly. Over the last ten years great world conferences have taken place on various crucial themes such as the Environment, Education, Population, Social issues and Women which have been attended by opinion makers of different backgrounds gradually weaving the fabric of a new global consciousness. The Vedanta in some ways is far ahead of the present level of human consciousness, a goal which we might perhaps be able to reach in another two or three centuries. But we have to reach if we are to have any kind of harmonious life on this planet in the future, because while science and technology have given us great miracles of space travel and other marvels, they have also given us tremendous destructive power which can easily destroy all life on planet Earth unless we develop the wisdom to match our knowledge. It is quite possible that this particular experiment in the evolution of consciousness could be brought to a violent end, there is no assurance that it will continue ad infinitum. Therefore, unless we take advantage of this wisdom, such as that in the Vedanta, we may find ourselves in great difficulty. This has its implications of course. If we really do believe that the human race is a single family, then we cannot exist in a family in which three members are starving to death and two are dying of over-eating. The family ultimately then has got to work as a family, and we have got to move towards a more sane, balanced and just global order. This concept has got to inform our actions increasingly as we move into the next century.

The fourth key concept in the Vedanta is of the essential unity of all religions—*Ekam sad viprah bahudha vadanti*, as the Rig Veda has it, the truth is one, the wise call it by many names. This pluralism is built into the very texture of Hindu thought. Long before the other religions of the world were born, Vedanta accepted many paths to the divine. You could go through a formless divine or you through divinity with form. When you come to a divinity with form, you have a whole choice, you can worship the divinity as a male or as a female, you can worship Shiva or Vishnu, Ganesha or Krishna, Hanuman or the Goddess, there is a whole spectrum of possibilities and no attempt to steamroll everyone into worshipping in exactly the same way.

This pluralism has to be the basis for the Interfaith movement that is developing in the world. We still find some religions claiming that they are the only and exclusive way to salvation, but that is prima facie unacceptable. How can we, creatures who happen to live on the tiny speck of dust called

Plant Earth, arrogate to ourselves the capacity to say that the all-pervasive divinity can manifest itself only in one way and at one time? Billions of people were born before that particular religion and billions will be born in other religions. Therefore the only sane approach is the acceptance of many paths to the divine, which is an essential feature of the Vedanta. That is what makes Vedanta so universal in its appeal. It holds that each individual can confront the divinity within or outside in a special way, because each one of us has got our own unique configuration, call it genetic or karmic, each one of us has got a unique consciousness and therefore it is open to us to move towards the divine in our own way. No religion has a monopoly of the truth, and though the followers of various religions can genuinely believe that theirs is the best, or even the only path to the divine, this does not give them the right to decry or denigrate other paths, far less to seek to impose their will through violence and coercion.

Within each religious tradition there is the concept of the inner light, "the light that lighteth every man that cometh into the world" as the Bible says, or the *Roohani Noor* of the Sufi mystics, or the *Ek Onkar* of the great Gurus. That light is within us, as Francis Thompson says in a marvellous poem:

Not where the wheeling systems darken,
And our benumbed conceiving soars—
The drift of pinions, would we hearken,
Beats at our own clay-shuttered doors.
The angels keep their ancient places;—
Turn but a stone, and start a wing!
'Tis ye, 'tis your estranged faces,
That miss the many-splendoured thing.

The many splendoured light of the Atman is not the preserve of any priest or any functionary, it resides within each human being. And so Vedanta is the greatest declaration of independence ever made, because it is our own *karma,* it is our own actions, it is the way in which we perceive the divine, it is the way in which we act out the drama of our lives, that will determine how our own consciousness develops and evolves.

The Vedanta is a very powerful statement of the Interfaith philosophy. There is a beautiful verse of the Mundaka Upanishad—

"As rivers in their flowing reach their destination in the ocean and there cast off their names and forms, so do those who have achieved divine realisation transcend all differences and realize the Great Being."

If there is a divinity that in fact informs the universe, it can appear in many ways but it cannot be the exclusive property of any particular formulation. This must become a very significant element of the new world consciousness that is emerging, and an essential pre-requisite for a harmonious global society. If in the name of religion, or in the name of particular beliefs, we are still going to indulge in conflict as has happened through history, disaster will ensue. It is astounding that while every religion looks upon its own manifestation of the divine as being compassionate, merciful and loving, yet in the name of that very divinity we have inflicted the most terrible horrors upon fellow human beings. This is something which can no longer continue in the global society. We must respect religious differences, but look upon them as a philharmonic orchestra with many different instruments being played, but all of them playing in harmony for the divine. That is what the Vedanta teaches us.

Fifth and finally, the Vedanta urges us to work for the welfare of all beings—*bahujana sukhaya bahujana hitayacha*—not only for individual salvation, but the welfare of society. Prayers in the Hindu tradition have never only been for personal welfare; but for the larger good. "May all beings be happy, may all be without disease, may all being perceive auspicious sights; may no-one suffer the pangs of sorrow." And again "May there be peace on earth, may there be the peace in the sky, may there be peace in the waters, may there be peace in the plants, in the trees; may there be peace in all celestial regions, may peace prevail everywhere." Thus we see that ecological values are built into the very structure of the Vedanta. The Atharva Veda has 63 extraordinary verses called the *Prithvi suktam,* or Hymn to the Earth which is possibly the most comprehensive statement of ecological and environmental values in any scripture. Vedanta believes in the divinity inherent in all manifestations, including the natural environment, and realizes that if we destroy the mountains, the forests, the oceans and the rivers, ultimately the human race is also destroyed. This linkage between human and natural environment is built into Vedanta, which does not accept that human beings have been given some kind of sovereignty to exploit all other forms of life on this planet.

In the Vedantic world view, this entire magnificent universe is permeated by the divine. The concept of *Bhavani Vasundhara,* Mother Earth, means that the earth manifests a divinity. It is this planet Earth that has nurtured consciousness up from the slime of the primeval ocean for billions of years to where we are today. What greater miracle could there be that from uni-cellular organisms we have developed today into beings who can break the space barrier, go to the moon, go to the planets, reach out to the stars. The greatest miracle is the miracle of human consciousness with its infinite capacities for growth and evolution.

These five concepts of the Vedanta—the all pervasive Brahman, the Atman that resides in all beings, the spiritual unity of the human race, the essential unity of all religions, and the welfare of all beings, if taken together, represent a global holistic philosophy which can sustain us in this tremendously important period of transition and turmoil through which humankind is passing. It is a philosophy that stresses convergence in place of conflict, cooperation in place of competition, holism in place of hedonism, and an interfaith dialogue in place of inter-religious wars. It is a philosophy that endows all human beings with a tremendous sense of potentiality and divinity.

It is not an easy path. Indeed it is a path beset with challenges and difficulties. But the Upanishads themselves remind us that we need a great deal of courage and compassion to reach the goal. It is not something that will come automatically. We have got to act—*charaiveti charaiveti*—to move against the current as it were, to move upwards. There are two dimensions of the human personality, the vertical dimension going inwards towards our spiritual essence, and the horizontal dimension going outwards to society. It is at the intersection of these that is found the source of our inner strength and our inner light.

The Katha Upanishad is one of the most eloquent and powerful texts where the boy Nachiketa goes to the hall of death and spends three nights and three days there, and then he is given three boons by

Yama. In the course of that extraordinary dialogue there is a verse which exhorts us to awake and to arise and to find out what the great seers in the past have taught and to move onwards across the razor-edged path. It is a difficult path beset with dangers, not simply the path of least resistance. There are no soft options left, either for individual greatness or for collective emancipation. But across that razor-edged path, endowed with the courage and compassion that Vedanta gives us, we can and must move towards the goal of a regenerated individual, of a regenerated society and of a compassionate and caring global society.

THE MUNDAKA UPNISHAD
THE BRIDGE TO IM-MORTALITY

Chapter 1

SECTION 1

1   Aum, Brahma, the creator of the universe, the protector of the world, arose before all the gods. He taught the knowledge of Brahman, which is the foundation of all knowledge, to his eldest son Atharvan.

2   The knowledge Atharvan imparted in ancient times to Angiras. He in turn taught it to Satyavaha, son of Bharadvaja, and the son of Bharadvaja passed it on to Angiras, the science thus descending from the greater to the lesser sages.

3   Shaunaka, the renowned householder, once approached Angiras with reverence in the manner laid down by the scriptures, and asked: 'Venerable Sir, what is that, knowing which, everything becomes known?'

4   To him Angiras replied: 'The knowers of Brahman declare that there are two kinds of knowledge to be acquired—the higher as well as the lower.

5   Of these the lower consists of the Rig-Veda, the Yajur-Veda, the Sama-Veda, the Atharva-Veda, phonetics, ritual, grammar, etymology, metrics and astronomy. And the higher is that by which the imperishable is attained.

6   That which is invisible, ungraspable, without origin or attributes, which has neither eyes nor ears, neither hands nor feet; which is eternal and many-splendoured, all-pervading and exceedingly subtle; that imperishable being is what the wise perceive everywhere as the source of creation.

7 As the spider sends forth and gathers in (its web), as herbs sprout upon the face of the earth, as hair grows upon the head and body of man, so from the immutable springs forth the universe.

8 By concentrated meditation, Brahman expands; from him matter is born, from matter life, mind, truth and immortality through works.

9 From Brahman, the all-seeing, the all-knowing, whose energy consists of infinite wisdom, from him is born Brahma, matter, name and form.

SECTION 2

1   This is the truth; the rituals which the seers beheld in the sacred hymns are elaborated in the three Vedas. Ye lovers of the truth, perform them constantly, for they are your paths to the world of good deeds.

2   When the sacred fire is well kindled and the flames begin to move, offer your oblations with faith between the two portions of fire.

3   For those whose fire sacrifice is not accompanied by the rites to be performed at the new moon and the full moon, at the four months of rain and at the first harvest, which is without guests and without offerings to all the gods, or which is performed contrary to scriptural injunctions; for such their hopes are destroyed in all the seven worlds.

4   The black, the fierce, the swift-as-mind, the crimson, the smoke-hued, the scintillating, the many-splendoured—these are the seven swaying tongues of the fire.

5   Whoever performs the rites and makes the offerings into these shining flames at the proper time, these in the form of the rays of the sun lead to where the lord of the gods resides.

6   The radiant ones cry, 'Come with us, Come with us', as they carry him up on the rays of the sun.

They speak pleasant words of sweetness and honour, saying 'This is the holy world of Brahman gained by your good work'.

7. Verily, frail are these rafts of the eighteen sacrificial forms, which represent only the inferior work. The ignorant who acclaim them as the highest good fall repeatedly into the domain of old age and death.

8. Though they consider themselves to be wise and learned, they are fools wandering aimlessly like the blind led by the blind.

9. Revelling in multifarious ignorance, such people think they have achieved the goal of life. But, being bound to passions and attachments, they do not attain knowledge and sink down in misery when

the effects of their good deeds are exhausted.

10   Such bewildered minds regard sacrifices and good works as most important and do not know any greater good. Having reaped in heaven their rewards of good deeds, they enter again this world or even a lower one.

11   But those who live in the forest leading a life of austerity and faith, tranquil, wise and keeping the mendicant's rule, they, purged of all impurities, go by the solar gate to where the immutable, imperishable being dwells.

12   Having examined the worlds gained by deeds, the wise seeker should become indifferent to them, for the eternal cannot be attained by work. To know that, let him approach with humility a guru who is

learned in the scriptures and established in the Brahman.

13.　　To such a seeker, whose mind is tranquil and senses controlled, and who has approached him in the proper manner, let the learned guru impart the science of Brahman through which the true, imperishable being is realized.

Chapter 2

SECTION 1

1

This is the truth. As from a blazing fire thousands of fiery sparks leap out, just so, my beloved, a multitude of beings issue forth from the imperishable and, verily, fall back into it again.

2

The divine being is formless, eternal and pure, pervading within and without, anterior both to life and mind. He transcends even the highest immutable.

3

From him are born life, mind and the senses; ether, air, fire, water and the all-supporting earth.

4   Fire is his head, the sun and moon his eyes, space his ears, the Vedas his speech, the wind his breath, the universe his heart. From his feet the earth has originated; verily he is the inner self of all beings.

5   From him comes the fire fueled by the sun; from the moon the rains which nourish herbs upon the earth. (Nourished by them) the male casts his seed into the female; thus are these many beings born of the divine being.

6   From him are born all Vedic hymns, of the Rig, Sama and Yajur, the sacrificial chants and the sacrifice; the ceremonies and the sacrificial gifts; the time of the sacrifice, the sacrificer and the world's purified by the moon and illuminated by the sun.

7   From him are born the many gods and celestial beings; men, beasts and birds, the in-drawn breath and the out-breath; rice and barley; austerity and faith, truth, chastity and the law.

8   From him also are born the seven senses; the seven flames and their fuel; the seven oblations and the seven worlds in which move the life-breaths; seven and seven which dwell in the secret place of the heart.

9   From him are all these mountains and oceans; from him the multifarious rivers flow; from him also are all the herbs and juices which, together with the elements, support the inner soul.

10   Verily, that great being is all this universe- sacrificial works, austerity and knowledge. O hand-

some youth, he who knows this immortal being as seated in the secret caverns of the heart cuts asunder the knot of ignorance even during this life on earth.

SECTION 2

1   The Brahman is the mighty foundation, manifesting deep in the secret cavern of the heart. In it are established all that breathe, and move and see. Know this both as being and non-being, as the supremely desirable, greatest and highest of beings beyond all understanding.

2   Luminious, subtler than the subtle, the imperishable Brahman is the abode of the worlds and all their peoples. It is life, it is speech, it is mind. It is reality and immortality. O beloved one, it is this which must be pierced; know it.

3   Having taken as a bow the great weapon of the secret teaching, one should fix in it the arrow sharpened by constant meditation. Drawing it with a mind filled with That (Brahman), penetrate, O good-looking youth, that imperishable as the mark.

4   The pranava (aum) is the bow; the arrow is the self; Brahman is said to be the mark. With heedfulness is It to be penetrated; one should become one with It as the arrow in the mark.

5   He in whom are in-woven the sky, the earth and interspace, alongwith the mind and all the life-breaths, know him as the one self and desist from other utterances. This is the bridge to immortality.

6   Where all the nerves and arteries come together like spokes of a chariot wheel at its hub, there,

moving within the heart, he becomes manifold.
Meditate on that self as aum; may your passage to
the other shore beyond the darkness be pleasant and
auspicious.

7   The omniscient, the all-wise, whose glory is
reflected here on earth, is the self enthroned in the
luminous city of Brahman, his etherial heaven.
Firmly established in mind, seated in the heart, he
controls life and body. The wise by the higher
knowledge see him clearly as the radiant, blissful,
immortal.

8   When the Great Being is seen as both the higher
and the lower, then the knot of the heart is rent
asunder, all doubts are dispelled and karma is
destroyed.

9　　In the highest golden sheath dwells the Brahman—stainless and indivisible. He is the light of all lights; it is he that the knowers of the self realize.

10　　There the sun does not shine, nor the moon and the stars; there these lightnings do not shine, how then this earthly fire? Verily, everything shines only after his shining; his shining illuminates this entire cosmos.

11　　Verily, the immortal Brahman is everywhere; in front and behind, to the north and the south, above and below; verily, Brahman alone is this great universe.

Chapter 3

SECTION 1

1   Two beautiful birds, closely bound in friendship, cling to a common tree. Of these one eats the delicious fruit with relish, while the other looks on without eating.

2   Seated on the same tree, one of them—the personal self—grieves on account of its helplessness. But when he sees the other—the worshipful lord in all his glory—then his sorrow passes away from him.

3 When the seer sees the golden-hued lord, the great being, who is the maker of the world and the source of Brahma the creator, then the wise one, shaking off good and evil, free from stain, attains unity with the Supreme.

4 Verily, it is the divine spirit that shines forth in all beings. Knowing this, the wise one desists from unnecessary talk. Sporting in the self, delighting in the self, yet involved in outer activity, such a one is the greatest among the knowers of Brahman.

5 The self within the body, pure and resplendent, is attained through the cultivation of truth, austerity, right knowledge and chastity. When their impurities dwindle, the ascetics behold him.

6   Truth alone triumphs, not untruth. By truth is laid out the divine path along which sages, their desires fulfilled, ascend to where truth has its supreme abode.

7   Vast, divine, beyond all thought processes shines the Brahman; subtler than the subtle, further than the furthest. Yet it is nearer than the nearest, and the seer sees it within the secret heart.

8   He cannot be grasped by the eye, by speech, nor by the other sense organs. Nor can be revealed by penance and austerities. Only when the mind becomes calm and purified by the grace of the higher knowledge does one, meditating, behold the great, indivisible being.

9   The subtle Atman within the body, pervaded by the five-fold life force, is to be known by thought. The mind is constantly pervaded by the senses; when it is purified, the self shines forth.

10   Whatever world the man of purified mind desires, whatever desires he wishes to fulfill, all these he attains. Therefore, let whoever is desirous of prosperity worship the man of self-realization.

SECTION 2

1. The man of self-realization knows the supreme Brahman upon which the universe is based and shines radiantly. The wise who, free from desire, worship the Brahman pass beyond the seed of rebirth.

2. Whoever in his mind longs for the objects of desire is born again and again for their fulfillment; but one whose desire for the Brahman is fully satisfied, for such a perfected soul all his desires vanish even here in this life.

3   Not by discourses, nor by intellectual analysis, nor through much learning can the *Atman* be attained. He is attained only by one whom he chooses; to such a one the Atman reveals its own form.

4   This self cannot be attained by one without strength, nor by the careless, not through improper austerities. But the wise who strive by all these means enter into the abode of Brahman.

5   Having attained the self the seers are fully satisfied with wisdom, perfect in their souls, non-attached and tranquil. Having realized the all-pervasive everywhere, these disciplined souls verily enter into the Brahman.

6   Firmly established in the Vedantic wisdom through the yoga of renunciation, their conscious-

ness purified, these seers at the end of time achieve immortality and liberation in the world of Brahman.

7   Gone are the fifteen parts into their foundations; the senses into the corresponding deities; the deeds and the intellect into the supreme, immutable being.

8   As flowing rivers disappear into the ocean, losing their separate name and form, even so the seer, freed from name and form, becomes one with the effulgent being, the highest of the high.

9   Verily, he who knows the supreme Brahman himself becomes Brahman. In his lineage none is born who knows not the Brahman. He crosses beyond sorrow, he crosses beyond sin. Liberated

from the knots of the heart, he becomes immortal.

10 This very doctrine is declared in the Vedic verse; to them alone who perform the rites, who are well versed in the scriptures, who are firmly grounded in the Brahman, who tend the sacred fire with devotion, who have duly performed the rite of the head, should this knowledge of the Brahman be imparted.

11 This is the truth imparted to his disciples in ancient times by the seer Angiras. Let no one who has not performed the rite study this. Salutations to the great seers! Salutations to the great seers!